HAIKU
FUCK YOU

JOSH MYERS

CB555-04: Haiku Fuck You
ISBN: 978-0-9962768-0-1
Library of Congress Control Number: 2015958979

Carrion Blue 555
Chicopee MA / Lambertville NJ
carrionblue555@gmail.com

"This is Heaven alright, but there's a man outside with a gun."
~Cardiacs, "What Paradise is Like"

This book was written in its entirety from November 17, 2015 — December 2, 2015, and is presented without further comment.

—Joseph Bouthiette Jr., editor

Dedicated to:
Joseph Bouthiette Jr. and Kaylee Stebbins,
the best friends a Champ could hope for.

HAIKU FUCK YOU

"Well, I haven't always been a perfect person
And I haven't done what mom & dad had dreamed
But on the day I die, I'll say
'At least I fucking tried!'
That's the only eulogy I need"

   —*Frank Turner, "Eulogy"*

Joseph
Your name is Joseph.
You are a fucking weirdo.
Joe is fucking dumb.

Josh
JOSH JOSH JOSH JOSH JOSH
JOSH JOSH JOSH JOSH JOSH JOSH JOSH
JOSH JOSH JOSH JOSH JOSH

MWM
I wrote Josh too much.
My name has lost all meaning.
It matches my life.

Hey, Go Fuck Yourself.
I wrote a haiku.
It's called "Hey, Go Fuck Yourself."
I'm so good at this.

I'm Really Good At This
I'm so good at this.
Like, I'm REALLY good at this.
Look how good I am.

Don't Interrupt My Dinner
I am eating food.
It is Middle Eastern food.
Now fuck off, you cunt.

The Haiku Champ
Josh is Haiku Champ.
Champion of haiku yes.
Josh Josh Josh Josh Josh.

Overreaction
You think I'm joking?
Motherfucker, I don't joke.
I will bury you.

Dare to Dream

They said I wasn't
the Champ I wanted to be.
But they can fuck off.

Thkullth

By the time I'm dead
I will achieve my life's goal:
I will be a skull.

#books #booklife #amreading

Books are really neat.
There are so many of them.
I like ones with guns.

Withered

Shop is now empty.
Blasting Electric Wizard.
What's the point of me.

Off to a Great Start
A one and a two
and now a haiku, fuck you,
this haiku is done.

Placeholder Title
I want to go home.
I am so tired right now.
Want to go to bed.

Yeah You
The sign on the door
says "Please: No Photos, No Phones."
That means you, fuckhead.

Fucking Try Me, Bouthiette
Joe wrote three haiku.
I wrote fifteen. Joe's a nerd.
Now I wrote sixteen.

Equality
Counting syllables,
I have to use my fingers.
I'm not good at math.

Joe is Dumb
Joe sweats writing these.
I don't understand why, though.
This is so easy.

Easiest Fucking Thing
Farley's Bookshop has
four syllables. That's alright,
because I have more.

Countdown
Using my fingers
to count syllables per line
is starting to hurt.

Toilet Time
A toilet haiku:
I am on the toilet now.
I made a mistake.

Night Night
Bed is where I sleep.
I like to sleep in my bed.
It is where I sleep.

Rules
I have a challenge:
Five hundred and fifty-five.
I'm a fucking pro.

Purpose
It has become clear:
this notebook is for haiku.
The future Bible.

Companionship
I have got a dog.
His name is Agent Cooper.
He is a good dog.

More Books
I have lots of books.
Big stacks all over the house.
I can't read them all.

Bootie-Tootie
Joe is my best friend.
We get along really well.
Even though he's dumb.

Pain?
My back hurts a bit.
Hunched over, writing haiku.
I should lie down soon.

Pride
I'm the Haiku Champ.
Ain't nobody can haiku
better than I can.

Inspiration
Anything is good
to write a haiku about.
Even writing one.

Wooo
This is how it's done.
Watch the champion at work.
Nothing stops this train.

Clean It On Up
My room is a mess.
I should really clean it up.
Maybe on Friday.

Oh No
I stress about books.
There are so many to read,
and I can't pick one.

Good Night
I should go to sleep.
I will write more tomorrow.
Haiku Champ for life.

Thinuth
My sinuses hurt.
They're giving me a headache.
I should take a pill.

No No No
Hold the fucking phone.
I started to think too much
about what to write.

JOSH MYERS

It's Sitting Right Over There
I should really read
that fat book of stories by
Clarice Lispector.

Bed Bed Bed Bed Bed
Don't want to get up.
I would like to stay in bed.
But I can't do that.

Personal
I wrote a haiku.
It's a haiku just for you.
It's called "Fuck Off, Dick."

Feelings
Take all your feelings,
wrap them up in a ball, and
shove them up your ass.

Wow I'm Good
Well hey there, bathrobe.
Ain't worn you in quite some time.
Wonder why that is.

A Perfect Gentleman
Kaylee is the best.
A precious baby angel.
Her name is not Kyle.

III
Will Pauley the third,
that bastard we call Williez,
tried to burn me twice.

Cooper, No
Cooper likes to lick.
His licking makes me angry.
I wish he would stop.

Look At the Time
Seven twenty-two
has five syllables and is
perfect for haiku.

Death 4 Ever
So "Octopope Death"
is also four syllables.
Boy, what a strange world.

Pattern Recognition
Oh no, I can't stop
thinking about syllables.
My brain is broken.

Undefeated
I already wrote
fourteen haiku this morning.
Fucking Haiku Champ.

Noise
Great big loud guitars
make me a happy chappy.
Pipe organs do, too.

Plane Against the Grain
As close to regret
as any of them come. I
wish that we still spoke.

Loop
Infinity loop
on my forearm, just to see
if I could take it.

Mutation
How is Mutation
on my leg a tribute to
what true friendship means?

Addicted
Symbol for music
that got me through a bad time.
That's up on my arm.

So It Goes?
For Kurt Vonnegut,
an asterisk on my arm.
Asshole on elbow!

Owls
Black Lodge or White Lodge?
I got this *Twin Peaks* tattoo
with my buddy Mike.

Rainy Day
Where is my raincoat?
Is it under all my shirts?
Yes. That is stupid.

THE QUESADILLA SUITE

HAIKU FUCK YOU

#1
Kaylee is eating
a quesadilla right now.
Eat that shit, Kaylee!

#2
Kaylee is a champ.
A quesadilla champ, son.
Best back the fuck up.

#3
Meat and cheese, I guess,
filled up the quesadilla.
Maybe some beans, too.

#4
Truth be told, I don't
eat quesadillas often.
So I have no clue.

#5
Flour tortilla
held the contents of the treat
that Kaylee just ate.

#6
Maybe it was rice
inside the quesadilla.
This is just guesswork.

#7
Or chicken, maybe?
That sounds more like our Kaylee.
Kyle is not her name.

#8
Fear and despair were
what filled the quesadilla
that Kaylee just ate.

#9
Or my hopes and dreams
in that ol' quesadilla.
I really don't know.

#10
What it was made of
is of little importance.
Kaylee is a champ.

#11
Quesadilla Champ
is what all the kids call her,
for she is the champ.

#12
That quesadilla
didn't stand a fucking chance
against Champ Kaylee!

#13
She ate the whole thing.
A whole damn quesadilla!
Three cheers for Kaylee!

#14
Have some respect, kid,
for the undisputed champ:
Kaylee forever!

#15
Kaylee is my friend.
She ate that quesadilla.
I am proud of her.

Lazy Twat
Joe went back to sleep.
He's a lazy fucking Joe.
He should be awake.

Breakfast
Breakfast lasagna
is the bestest lasagna.
You can all fuck off.

Nature
Fresh apple cider
is so fucking delicious.
I drink it a lot.

Genuine
Ironic writing
is the worst thing in the world.
Write with heart or die.

Genuine 2
And yeah, I get it.
This seems pretty ironic.
But I'm having fun.

Genuine 3
Hell, this is the most
I've written of anything
in months. This is real.

Hygiene
Brush your fucking teeth
or they'll rot and break and hurt.
I should get dentures.

Money
Paycheck tomorrow.
I waste money all the time.
Need an accountant.

Accounting
I could get that new
Wildhearts Christmas sweater, but
it is expensive.

Found Haiku
Live Twitter chat and
video release, Thursday,
November nineteenth.

Ingenuity
How lazy is that?
Just take some words from an ad
and make a haiku.

Hairy Situation! Yuk Yuk Yuk
I need a haircut,
but I'm growing my hair out.
What a dilemma!

Clothes
I have to get dressed.
Pick out a good shirt for work.
Eraserhead tee!

Poor Planning
I didn't bring food.
I don't have cash for pizza.
Guess I'll go hungry.

Salvation
Oh wait, I forgot!
There's cheese in the upstairs fridge!
Ha ha ha, I win.

Overanalyzing
Josh is who I am,
I sometimes write stupid shit,
and my name is Josh.

Pay Them Bills
Toilet time at work.
I'm getting paid to write this.
That is pretty rare.

Rainy Dayny
Rainy day at work.
Hardly any customers.
I do not mind this.

But I Don't Care Why Anymore
In the work bathroom.
There is bleach under the sink.
And I don't know why.

The Braggart
THE CHAMP IS BACK, SON.
HAIKU CHAMP WILL NEVER DIE.
I AM ETERNAL.

Call an Ambulance
Jesus fucking Christ.
Can you believe these haiku?
I'm on fucking fire.

Close Alone
Back in five minutes
while I go use the restroom.
Deal with it, bitches.

I'm Serious
Cat food is awful.
It smells like the depths of Hell.
Glad I have a dog.

Happiness and Joy
Hot cocoa at work
from my Cardiacs mug, while
rain pours down outside.

What Am I Doing
Spider on the door
I pretend is my best friend.
I call him José.

BFF
I have this one friend,
Stephanie M. Wytovich,
whose writing is class.

JFFVRT
I know someone else,
Joseph Bouthiette Jr.,
who is fucking dumb.

Leaky Times
Sometimes the roof leaks.
I hope it doesn't tonight.
That would really suck.

Sick Burn
Face it, Bouthiette.
I just write better than you.
Can't beat the Champ, dawg.

Hunnert
One hundred haiku
in only two days? Hot damn!
I'm so good at this.

Not Yet
It's pissing down rain.
I hope it slows down by nine.
Not fun to drive in.

With Respect to Mr. Jokes
Want to hear a joke?
Hey! Get up on outta here!
This is my bathroom!

Stained Class
A stain on the floor
looks like a wonky dondle
and it made me laugh.

Sacred Patience
Work is fucking dead.
Playing *Sing to God* all night.
Helps to pass the time.

Crawling Towards Nine
I want to be home.
I will have a nice cold beer
and write more haiku.

Thursday Strikes Again
Throwing treats at cat.
Fuck all this Thursday bullshit.
One's stuck on his back.

Classiest of the Classy
A bathroom haiku
by Joshua M. Myers.
Poop dee doop dee doop.

A Birthday Haiku For David W. Barbee
Hey, David Barbee.
Today is your birthday, right?
Happy birthday. Josh.

Seventh Son
Captain Maniac,
oh dear Captain, my Captain.
What's the point of you?

Of a Seventh Son
Through all of my life,
I've been waiting here for you,
Captain Maniac.

Returns
Just got home from work.
Time to get some mac and cheese
with barbeque sauce.

Tarnation!
Nothing like a beer
after a long day at work
to something something

STEBBINS
Kaylee is so cool.
Kaylee is my favorite.
She is my hero.

Bestest
Look, I'm not joking.
I aspire to be as cool
as Kaylee just is.

Farley's
I do love my job,
though customers can be shit.
But I am home now.

Joe Joe
For all I mock him,
Joseph Bouthiette Jr.
is my bestest pal.

And None Too Happy
Coughing dog woke me
at three forty-five a.m.
Now I am awake.

Tart Fart
I just wrote a 'T'
that looked a lot like an 'F'.
Abandon all hope.

Hooray!
I like doing these.
It makes writing fun again.
Better not fuck up.

Backlit
Song stuck in my head:
"Backlit" by Sequence of Prime.
I'm not complaining.

Desk
I should clean my desk
so I can use it again.
But I'd need a chair.

Dilemma!
Desk chairs are pricy.
I don't get paid all that much.
Though I could steal one.

Sneaky
My new sneakers are
not actually that new.
They're falling apart.

Metaphor
It's like this one thing
really means, like, something else.
How deep is that, bro.

Abstract
My sister made me
a blanket from scraps of yarn.
It makes me happy.

4:18
I am still awake.
I should go back to sleep now.
That is a good plan.

4:21
After this haiku
I will try to get more sleep.
Good night, good morning.

Waidmanns Heil
There's a Rammstein song
where it sounds like Till's yelling
"STEBBINS" for Kaylee.

Hey Hey
I'm pretty awkward,
and I don't like it at all.
But what can you do?

Lunchtime
Today's lunch will be
fuckin' rigatoni and
motherfuckin' sauce.

Sauced
My favorite sauce
is Manoff Market Gardens'.
It's so fucking good.

More Sauce
Seriously, guys.
Stuff it in your goddamn face.
It's that fucking good.

Time Management
Day off poorly spent.
Haven't written all that much.
But went to get sauce.

Quite Interesting
Watching *QI* now,
writing occasionally,
not nearly enough.

HAIKU FUCK YOU

Pens!
I doubt that this pen
will last through all these haiku.
Good thing I have more.

So Fuck Off
Serious writing
might be considered better,
but this is more fun.

NCBC4LIFE
Neshaminy Creek
makes very good beer and is
run by my cousin.

How About It
Didn't mean to drink,
but this beer was in the fridge,
so there you have it.

Larry
Joe has a houseguest
and his name is Laurance, but
I call him Larry.

Inetllect
I buy stuff from the
Criterion Collection
to make me feel smart.

Good Start
I went to breakfast
with my grandfather today.
That was very nice.

Bathroom Musings 1
A pretty bathroom
is kind of funny to me
'cause that's where you poop.

Bathroom Musings 2
Poop isn't pretty.
Unless you're into that stuff.
In which case, sorry.

Advice Corner
Act like an adult,
ignore all of your problems,
and die too early.

Shower Power
Shower ideas
are sometimes not the worst ones
you will have that day.

Introduction
Hi, my name is Josh.
I write this kind of bullshit.
Now leave me alone.

Rhythm
Haiku has rhythm
thanks to a unique system
of fucking about.

Fancy Bathroom
Fancy bathroom man.
I just pissed in this bathroom.
Fancy fancy Josh!

Hairy Joe
Joe shaved his dumb head.
But he didn't shave his beard.
Joe has a big beard.

Oh No Joe
Joe's beard is too big.
Guess I could set it on fire.
But it might hurt him.

Mead!
I do not like wine,
but I'm a fan of good mead.
That's okay by me.

The Fat Friar
A guy up in Maine,
a guy called the Fat Friar,
makes delicious mead.

Like a Stupid Baby
Joe's noggin is bald,
just like a stupid baby.
Joe is a baby.

Stupid Baby
Bald Joe. Bald bald bald.
Do you see how bald he is?
He's so fucking bald.

Friend Joe
I make fun of Joe
because he is my best friend.
Fucking stupid twat.

Disappointed
Didn't read today.
I don't feel good about that.
In fact, I am sad.

Friday
I write this haiku
sitting tired on the couch.
Fascinating stuff.

Surrealism, I Guess?
Toothbrush commercial.
But why are they brushing corn?
What the fuck is that?

Paaaaants
My pants are dirty.
I've only worn them four days.
What a fucking joke.

Pillowth
Leaning on pillows
to write haiku in my bed
sort of hurts my back.

Get Ready For Sleeptime
Time for pajamas.
They're really just a t-shirt
and my underwear.

Ol' Pillercase
My pillow is old
and discolored from my head,
but I still use it.

Hey You
Judge me all you want,
airing this personal shit.
I don't give a fuck.

Really?
I still can't believe
that I'm writing all this shit
and enjoying it.

No Help
SubRosa's album,
No Help For the Mighty Ones,
sure is fuckin' nice.

Embarrassing If This Ever Gets Published
Writing while pooping.
Haiku as message to Joe.
My life is a joke.

HAIKU FUCK YOU

Friends As Friends
I'm not religious.
If I were, I'd go Quaker.
They seem like good folk.

Dictation
Messaging Joseph
haiku that I write while I
sit on the toilet.

Fucking Why
I'm not even drunk.
It's just fun to write this shit.
I still don't know why!

Fuck You, Bouthiette
Spiffy haiku, bro.
But did you write fifty-five?
I did just today.

Get Well Soon, Timmy
Tim Smith. Cardiacs.
Best music in all the world.
Absolute beauty.

New Day Rising
I have work at three.
It is now seven forty.
Lots of time to write.

Where is Joe?
Joe is still asleep.
Joe is a lazy bastard.
I write more than him.

Joe is Asleep!
How much can I write
before Joe wakes the fuck up?
I bet quite a bit.

HAIKU FUCK YOU

Lazy Fucking Joe
That's already three.
More than Joe will write today.
The lazy bastard.

He Should Wake Up
This is how you write.
You write like a goddamn pro.
Like the Haiku Champ!

But He Won't, Because He's Lazy
That's five for today
and Joey is still asleep.
Haiku 'til I die.

SUPER$HIT666
Wake up with loud tunes.
Big guitars and harmonies.
Joe is still asleep!

My God, He's Still Asleep!
Joe is still asleep.
Do you think he's still asleep?
He is still asleep.

Big Sleeping Baby
All cozy in bed
with his dumb head all shaved
like a big baby.

What If He's Dead?
Maybe he is dead.
That would sure be a letdown.
Hey, don't be dead, Joe.

Hey Look, It's My Dog
Cooper is a goof.
A big ol' weirdo goof dog.
Joe is still asleep.

OH SHIT HE WOKE UP

Hey! Joe is awake!
Which means that he is not dead.
Lazy fucking Joe.

Charlie

Charlie sure loves math.
He maths all the fucking time.
I am bad at math.

JIF

Does Kaylee like Jen?
Wait, everybody likes Jen.
Because Jen is great.

Fingernails

Fingernails are dumb.
I hate having to clip them.
But clip them I must.

Golly Gee Wow
Mac and cheese breakfast
with leftover mac and cheese.
I will be dead soon.

Me Me Me
I need a shower.
I have work in five hours.
I have lots of time.

Please
Can I go to Maine?
Pack all my shit and leave now.
Next year is too far.

Aw, Heck
Only two dollars
in my poor little wallet.
I should hit the bank.

Clarification
I won't rob the bank,
I meant use the ATM,
take some money out.

Post-Payday
Got paid yesterday.
I could buy so much dumb shit.
I really shouldn't.

Shopping
It's about time to
start buying Christmas presents.
Hope you all like books.

Me Me Me Me
Really should shower.
I've just been sitting right here,
writing dumb haiku.

Read More
I should read today.
I didn't read yesterday.
And that still bugs me.

Magus
The Magus is great,
but I've become obsessed with
these stupid haiku.

Necessity
Haiku out of need
to write another haiku.
This is a haiku.

Holy Smokes, Dude
Also a haiku
is this, what I'm writing now.
Can you believe it?

Two Hunnert
Two hundred haiku
in only four goddamn days.
I'm the Haiku Champ!

Bark Bark
"Oxide Dog" is just
three syllables. Put that in
your pipe and fuck off.

Clout
When driving to work,
I like to blast good music
to scare the tourists.

Two Hours
Work in two hours
and I'm here doing fuck all.
My brain does not work.

Butter
Yes, the cat's still here.
No, I don't know where he is.
We sell books here, sir.

Butter 2
The cat is asleep.
I will not get him for you.
Fuck off out of here.

Bags, Yo
Stamping shopping bags
with an old Farley's logo
is hurting my hand.

Hey Kid
Caitlyn's on her phone,
looking at Pinterest shit.
No one gives a fuck.

Charlie No
Charlie's good at math.
He likes to do math problems.
They make my head hurt.

Hell No
Taking pictures of
books to go buy somewhere else?
Fuck off out my shop.

Why, Charlie?
Charlie's dinner time.
He fucking abandoned us.
Charlie, you bastard.

Slow On Down
Work always dies down
when it's around dinner time.
That's okay with me.

Dinner Time
I used "dinner time"
in two haiku in a row.
It's three syllables.

Poots
I'm the best at this.
Writing haiku at work now.
I'm the fucking Champ.

Colden Times
Caitlyn sure is cold.
It's all that she's been saying.
She should get a coat.

Customers
Shitty customers
make my soul cry out, "FUCK OFF."
Just be cool, assholes.

I Heart New York. Only Joking. Ha Ha.
Tourists from New York
are the bane of our work life.
They refuse to die.

The Champ Strikes Again
Caitlyn is leaving.
She can't handle the thunder
brought by my haiku.

Perfume
Way too strong perfume
is making my eyes water.
Please leave now, lady.

What is That
Something smells like fart.
It is really really bad.
I want it to stop.

Mystery!
Was it Caitlyn or
was it a customer or
did the cat do it?

STANK
Way too many smells
going on in the bookshop.
I do not feel well.

Mr. Wizard
Charlie is still gone.
What if he never comes back?
Who would show me math?

Don't Panic
Charlie just came back.
I don't have to call the cops.
Crisis averted.

CHAMPEEN
I haiku dumb shit,
but I do it very well.
That's why I'm the Champ.

Pro-fuckin'-fessional
Who am I kidding,
I don't do this well at all.
I just write a lot.

Water Bottle
My water bottle
has lots of stickers on it,
and I put them there.

Secret Like
I thought you'd like that.
A peek into my work space.
Now fuck off, hippie.

Work Tunes
We play jazz a lot,
and that is okay by me.
I've come to like jazz.

Haiku Bullshit
This is so easy,
anybody could do it.
But I am the Champ!

Mathematical
Charlie's a wizard.
He does math problems real good.
I cannot subtract.

Thanks, Charlie
I don't like Hitler.
He was a very bad guy.
My shoe is untied.

Coltrane
A Love Supreme now.
Coltrane to get through the night.
This will do nicely.

Almost Done Work
Fifty-five minutes
left of my work shift today.
I'm in the bathroom.

Nice and Warm Like
Radiator's on.
Keeps me nice and warm in here
while I am pooping.

This Morning
Typing up haiku.
I wrote a bunch yesterday
while I was at work.

Yes, You Look Like a Goddamn Murderer
You look like a cunt.
Look at your bald fucking head.
I miss my old friend.

Lord of the Flies
My "Fly Pope" t-shirt
is risky to wear to work.
I do anyway.

Another Shirt
Sing to God shirt, too,
gets me some weird looks at work.
But it's a great shirt.

Lansdale
Reading Joe Lansdale
is always a goddamn treat.
That man is the man.

French Bakery
Starbucks can fuck off.
C'est La Vie is where it's at.
Support good people.

Hide and FUCK OFF.
Don't play hide and seek.
This is a fucking book shop.
Get out. Get out now.

Shut the Fuck Up
All My Friends Are Dead
needs to join all of its friends
in a fucking pit.

Get the Fuck Out
I don't give a shit
that you came just to see him,
the cat is asleep.

Long Islanders
Where did you come from?
Why on earth did you come here?
Why won't you go home?

Seriously, Go Away
Ask about the cat.
The dumbest fucking questions.
WOULD YOU PLEASE GET OUT.

These Guys
Buffy and Charlie
are who I am working with.
Charlie. And Buffy.

I Mean It Now.
Get out of my shop,
you awful fucking dickhead.
Get the fuck out now.

HAIKU FUCK YOU

Angry Time
Some angry haiku
to reflect my angry soul.
Fuck you. Fuck right off.

I Beg You, SHUT UP
Loud people outside.
Want to hit them with hammers
so they go quiet.

Silence, Cat
Holy fuck, Butter.
It's not time to eat just yet.
Stop yelling at us.

Loudness Wars
Everything is loud.
I feel like I'm hungover
without being drunk.

Fender Lizards
Break from *The Magus*
to read Joe Lansdale's new book.
Fucking brilliant.

Poopin' Haiku
Indian dinner
left me with a happy gut,
but the bathroom calls.

Poopin' Haiku Number Two
Here on the toilet,
making some horrible sounds,
I question my life.

**I Don't Know How to Process Most
Emotions, and Rely On Poor Attempts At
Humor to Compensate For It.**
It's warm in here, though.
Forgot about the heater
sitting next to me.

HAIKU FUCK YOU

Huffy Bastings
Buffy thinks that I
should write serious poems,
but he knows better.

You've Known Me For Too Long
He knows that I'm dumb,
just pretends not to notice.
What a pal he is.

Dear Joe
I fucking hate you.
That there is five syllables.
So go fuck yourself.

THE PHILADELPHIA SEXTET

HAIKU FUCK YOU

#1
Philadelphia.
I hear people say "Philthy."
And now I know why.

#2
Sirens all the time.
A screaming chorus at night.
Such a warm welcome.

#3
Philly scared the shit
out of me, and that's the truth.
But we made it, guys!

#4
Kaylee had a knife,
and even though it was small,
it was still something.

#5
Sleeping on the floor
in Joe and Kaylee's bedroom
fucked my back right up.

#6
But still, all in all,
I had a pretty great time.
Glad we didn't die.

B.E. Burkhead
He's loud as all hell,
but funny as shit and one
beast of a poet.

Need Sleep
I writed haiku.
Wroted haiku yes Josh yes.
Josh haiku yes Josh.

All Them Troubles
Yesterday was off.
Didn't write many haiku,
and they weren't that good.

Monday Mornin'
Work in five hours.
Closing by myself tonight.
Haiku shall be wrote.

JOSH MYERS

Air-Conditioned Nightmare
It sure is quiet
when I shut off the A.C.
I HEAR EVERYTHING.

Zero Hero, Hey Hey
Bad Idea Man
is my superhero name.
Nope, nope, and away!

Five Five Five
I dreamed about a
555 eight-track cartridge.
I might drink too much.

Just Listing Things In My Field of Vision Now
Eraserhead tape
with Japanese subtitles
from my pal Mike Nau.

Inspirational
Dog bone. Stack of books.
Haiku about anything.
Who gives a rat's ass?

Son of Doop
Cooper is snoring,
which is better than
telling me to kill.

Friend Pal
A haiku for Joe:
Hey Joe. Hey Joe. Hey Joe. Joe.
Hey Joe. Hey. Fuck off.

What a Friend
Haiku for Williez:
I'll write you five syllables:
one two three fuck you.

Best Ever Friend
Haiku for Kaylee:
Kaylee is a gentleman.
Quesadilla Champ!

Also Stephanie
Haiku for Wyto:
Your happiness makes me sick.
High five, BFF.

Oh, Him.
A haiku for Matt:
Why must you be upside-down?
We need to hang out.

Okay, Done
Those are all my friends.
I don't know anyone else.
Just those five people.

HAIKU FUCK YOU

Asymmetrical
Cooper's ears are weird.
One goes straight up. The other,
well, the other don't.

Fuck You
Relative Rates of
Radical Bromination
is really a thing.

No Idea What They're In For
Highlight of my day:
a blind sale of *Hitler* by
D. Harlan Wilson.

Beardy Idiot
Joe's beard is real big.
I'm not jealous at all, though.
I don't care one bit.

Chris
Joe knows this one guy
who is his lab partner, Chris.
Joe thinks he is Paul.

Hey Chris
Joe thinks Chris is Paul.
Be fair, he looks like a Paul.
But he is a Chris.

Not Paul!
Chris is not Paul, Joe.
You know that, Joe. You know that.
Try to remember.

Rememberizational Exercise
Think it with your brain:
Chris is not Paul. Chris. Not Paul.
Use your thinker, Joe.

HAIKU FUCK YOU

Hey Pal
Tell Chris I say hi,
and that he looks like a Paul,
but he is a Chris.

Wait
Or is his name Paul
and you think his name is Chris?
I don't understand.

Hang On
What is that guy's name?
Is it Paul or is it Chris?
Which is the right one?

I Can't Stand the Confusion In My Mind
He looks like either,
if I'm being honest here.
Just call him "you there."

A Plan
Call him that until
he says his real name again.
I think it is Paul.

An Explanation
He looks like a Paul,
I don't know, he's your lab guy.
You figure it out.

I'm Losing My Temper
Why's this involve me?
I don't even know the guy,
Chris or whatever.

Stop It
I really don't care.
Chris or Paul, does not matter.
It's not my problem.

That's Enough
You tell this fucker,
next time you see him, from me:
get a better name.

No More
Haiku something else.
Not this name-swapping demon.
Life goes on, Joey.

Power
Cat wants his dinner,
and I'm the only one here.
I have become GOD.

Corrupts
Dance for me, Butter.
Entertain your God for food.
Gee, your claws are sharp.

And a Short Silence
Playing Cardiacs
on the loudspeakers at work
is a lovely thing.

Click! Run!
It does my heart good
to play music I adore
in a place I love.

Farley's Bookshop
This place is special.
Not to get all sappy-like,
but I like it here.

Cat Sick Blues
What did I just watch?
I need to go outside now.
Cat Sick Blues, you win.

HAIKU FUCK YOU

Shame
Hardly wrote today.
I do better when busy.
Days off are too lax.

Yep
Been in a weird mood.
Angry at dumb shit today.
Not good for haiku.

How About That
Well, wrote two haiku
about not writing haiku,
and one about them.

None
I'm not inspired,
I'm just really really dumb.
What's the point of this.

Exactly
I guess there's not one.
There's liberation in that.
No bullshit, just... this.

Honesty?
It's pretty honest,
in a real dumb kind of way,
writing anything.

Truth
No matter how dumb,
like this one I'm writing now,
it stands as valid.

Huh.
Did I find the point
over halfway through this thing?
Did it just take doubt?

Okie Doke
It feels pretty good
now that that's out of the way.
Maybe. Probably.

Done Fuck All
I had the day off.
Watched a very strange movie
and ran some errands.

7:24 pm
Saved haiku writing
until the end of the day.
Better than nothing.

Lost Themes
"Write haiku about
John Carpenter's *Lost Themes*," is
what Joe said to do.

Carpenter
It's a great album,
I'm just not sure what to write
other than, "It good."

Revert
Matthew Revert is
one of the best dudes around.
Everyone loves Matt.

3 min
Why did you text me
"3 min," oh father of mine?
What does it all mean?

Woo, Don't Get Crazy Now
Eating yogurt and
hanging out with ol' Cooper.
I'm livin' it up.

HAIKU FUCK YOU

It's Great
Matt is showing me
potential covers for this
bullshit I'm writing.

Late Day
Woke up late today.
Haven't done much this morning.
Work is in a bit.

Tomorrow
Writing dumb haiku.
Tomorrow is Thanksgiving.
I won't have to work.

Black Friday
But then, Black Friday.
I've got work. I just hope the
body count is low.

Call a Doctor
I called Joe "Joe-dawg."
I don't know what's happening.
Am I sick? Dying?

A Discussion
This got out of hand.
This was all meant as a joke!
Why is this a book?

Stupid Josh
Running out of steam?
That doesn't sound like the Champ!
The Haiku Champ lives!

Fucking Hell, Kill Me
Matt's covers are great,
but not enough for the Champ!
The best for the Champ!

Goddammit, No.
Haiku Champ haiku:
I'm better than all of you!
I'm better than me!

Champ Pants
People telling me
to write serious poems.
I tell them, "Fuck off."

Fucking Joe
Joe's not helping me.
I'm out of ideas, but
that won't stop the Champ!

Hey Bud
A quick haiku for
Joseph Bouthiette Jr.:
Go fuck yourself, Joe.

Fuck You, Shitbird.
Joe don't give a shit.
I can call him every name
and he just smiles.

Bootie-Tootie #2
It gets annoying.
I genuinely hate him,
and he won't fuck off.

Disgraceful
I asked Joe for help
but his suggestions are shit.
He's just a disgrace.

Peasants
Talking shop with Joe
via messages while I'm
here on the toilet.

Constitutional
My life has gone weird.
A haiku in the bathroom.
Are you reading this?

DON'T FORGET YOUR FOOD
Hope I don't forget
to bring food to work again.
That shit sucks real hard.

Turn Your Shit Around!
Is your life a mess?
Turn it around with haiku!
Only thirteen bucks!

Long Unders
Oh, long underwear.
You stop my legs being cold
and warm up my bits.

JOSH MYERS

I Really Do Hate Parking
The work parking lot
is a fucking nightmare, since
I can't park for shit.

Eskimo
Drinking and playing
The Residents' *Eskimo*.
This is my job, guys.

Cat Freaks
Fuck off, you dipshit.
We're not a petting zoo, kid.
We sell books, you know.

Eskimo 2
Nobody likes you.
Leave the shop. Album is weird.
We won't stop for you.

HAIKU FUCK YOU

Wednesday
Tonight does not suck.
Beer, good tunes, and a good friend.
I love my job. Thanks.

Dear Joe,
I think the best, mate.
I'm the fucking Haiku Champ!
I'll knock your ass out!

Dumb Bullshit
Something something Joe.
That fucker's not worth my time.
I'm the goddamn Champ!

Teens
I hate teenagers.
I'd like to burn all of them,
but that's illegal.

FUCK OFF OUT OF HERE
Play "Faster Than Snakes"
to drive these fucking kids out.
Great song, but not kind.

Work Haiku, Fuck You
Charlie is reading.
And I'm writing about it.
What is he reading?

Spooky Action
Some nerd book, you know.
Something that smart people like.
Those people are nerds.

Smarty Pants
Something sciencey.
You think you're better than me?
I'm the Haiku Champ!

I Win, Smart Guy
Sure, you can do math.
I can write haiku, bitches.
I win everything!

I Wish I Could Do Math
Haiku is useful!
Not like dumb old math, Charlie.
Haiku is smarter!

Numbers Freak Me Out
Who uses math, huh?
Just nerds and other dumb nerds.
Haiku's where it's at!

I Feel Inadequate
Haiku is so cool.
It gets me laid all the time.
Haiku sex machine!

Sorry, Yo.
That was all a lie.
I'm no haiku sex machine.
I'm the Haiku Champ!

I FUCKING WIN
How do you like that?
Motherfuckin' Champ got you!
Five-seven-five, bitch!

Job Insecurity
Bosses might read this.
I hope I don't get fired.
I love my job, guys.

So Many Ads. It's Just One Big Ad.
Well, TV must die.
The Thanksgiving Day parade
has become torture.

Ow Balls Ow
Coop jumped on my balls.
Why did that make me feel sick?
Because it sure did.

Stuffing
Just ate more stuffing.
Man, I shouldn't have done that.
I should go to bed.

The Triumphant Return
Took yesterday off
from writing haiku, but now
the Haiku Champ's back!

Black Windows
Working Black Friday.
Twelve to eight today, and then
I'm there all weekend.

Preparation
This will be a test
to see if I'm prepared for
Christmastime madness.

Tourism
Any rude tourists
will get haiku in their face.
Don't fuck with the Champ!

Ding Dong
We need a hammer
or a huge wooden mallet
to hit tourists with.

Gotta Get Up, Son
Calm down about work.
I don't leave for three hours.
Really need to piss.

So Much Stuffing
Bed sure is comfy,
but the bathroom is calling.
Thanksgiving payback.

Angurgapi
Icelandic symbol
to keep barrels from leaking.
Whatever, I'm Josh.

Birthday Trouble
Jen Farley's birthday.
I didn't get her a thing.
Maybe wine? Wine's good.

Hooray For Booze!
Everyone likes booze.
It's the perfect birthday gift,
says the Haiku Champ!

Happy Joshmas
Well, hey. I like booze,
and I'm pretty damn smart, so
booze must be the best.

Can't Piss In Bed, It's Unseemly
I am still in bed.
I am still dying to pee.
When will I get up?

A Promise to YOU
After this haiku,
I will get up and go piss,
then write about it.

It Just Kept Coming
I did it. I'm back.
That was a very long piss,
I don't mind saying.

No No No No No
Black Friday haiku
to ward off the bad people:
FUCK OFF, BAD PEOPLE.

England Keep My Bones
Hearing new music
that gets you all excited
is just wonderful.

Breakfast Eggs
Had eggs for breakfast
at ten twenty-eight a.m.,
with goat cheese and toast.

On a Roll
Might need a new pen
in case this one runs out while
I'm on a roll, yo.

Fascinating! Wow!
Might rain this weekend.
Interesting stuff! Whoa shit!
Quality haiku!

Sweet Heaven, Save Me From That Candle
It's busy at work.
The shop is full of tourists,
the stench of hellfire.

Hide Nowhere
Seek blessed relief
hiding in the shop bathroom.
They can't get me here.

Change Gears
Great friends. New tunes. Dog.
Good things that keep me grounded.
Write something else, Josh.

HAIKU FUCK YOU

YOU FUCKIN' WHAT
Ha ha ha, fuck off.
I'm the Haiku Champ, bitches!
Don't need no groundin'!

Let's Talk About Joe
Joe's a fucking nerd
and everybody knows it.
Look at Joe! Dumb nerd!

Sorry, Joe
Sorry for that, pal.
I shouldn't make fun of you.
You dumb fucking twat.

More About Joe
Joe's bald fucking head
is like an upside-down guy
with a beard for hair.

what
Not sure what that meant.
Whatever, look at his head.
It is fucking BALD.

Zero Saints
Bought a book today
by my good pal Gabino.
It looks fucking cool.

The Champagne of Beers
Miller High Life, dude.
Not drinking it right now, but
it sure is nice stuff.

High Life
People give it shit,
like it's not respectable.
It's my go-to beer.

Hey, Fuckhead
If you don't like it,
you can stick your opinion.
It's good beer, fuck off.

Self Defense
Cardiacs t-shirt
worn in defense against the
fucking heathen tide.

Preparation
Taking a six-pack
to work this afternoon so
we can steel ourselves.

We Shall Defeat Our Enemies
Winter IPA
to arm us against the whores
who would see us dead.

And Run the Streets Red
Charlie and myself,
just us, six to eleven,
and we shall triumph.

A Warning
All sirens downtown,
no doubt caused by the tourists
who can't FUCKING DRIVE.

Memory of Road Rage
Fucking yield, lady.
This is how New Yorkers die,
you fucking shithead.

This is New Jersey
You're in the country,
not the Jersey from TV.
Behave or die, scum.

HO HO HO MOTHERFUCKER
Oh, Christmas shopping?
Fuck that, I'm the Haiku Champ!
I bring you haiku!

Roger
I called Joe "Roger"
and I thought it was funny.
Disagree? Tough shit.

Can't Spell "Paint" Without "Ain't"
Painting the kitchen.
Golly, those sure are some fumes.
Champ's gettin' dizzy.

Belated Introductions
Hello there. I'm Josh.
This is Cooper. He's my dog.
Him have got four legs.

Pointless
I could be reading.
Instead, here I am writing.
Like a fucking Champ.

Yes, That's Sarcasm
Reading's for losers.
Unless you are reading this.
Then you're a champ, champ.

Laws
People who don't read
can't and shouldn't be trusted.
Oh. Unless they're blind.

Haiku In Braille
Wait, no. Braille, bitches.
No excuse not to read, then.
Unless you are dead.

Spooky Time
Hang on, can ghosts read?
Ghosts aren't real, you knucklehead.
What am I doing.

I Feel Like I Already Wrote This
I will blast metal
in my car, to and from work,
to scare off tourists.

Lookin' Cloudy
Might write at work if
we're not insanely busy.
Maybe it will rain.

Food For Today!
Taking more stuffing
to have later on at work.
It's made with apples.

Really Really Good
No lie, faithful pals,
stuffing with apples is great.
Fucking delicious.

Shut Up, Joe
Joe said hurry up
so he can edit and shit.
I'll do what I want.

Seriously, Joe. Shut Up.
Why edit this stuff?
It's all solid gold, fucker.
Cut, print, that's a wrap!

The Champ, the Champ!
I've just been thinking:
This sure is a dumb project.
But it's loads of fun.

Preposterous
Pretty cloudy out.
Maybe we WILL get that rain.
That would be a treat.

This is Fuckin' Dumb
Wash the stink of those
horrible tourist fuckers
from this fair city.

Time
Almost one o'clock,
which means work in two hours,
but I leave early.

Listen Here
I mean I leave here
early in case of traffic.
Just to clear that up.

Yeah Yeah Yeah
Beer at work later,
plus some stuffing. With apples.
Not a bad plan, Champ.

Mileage
Another haiku
about Joe's big dumb bald head.
Boy, it sure i bald!

Long-Term Goals
Still writing haiku.
Will I stop after my goal?
Will I be able?

Yowza
Not too long before
five hundred and fifty-five.
Faster than I thought.

HAIKU FUCK YOU

Stupid Idiot
This all came about
thanks to my dumb ideas
and Joe's love of them.

The Champ is the Champ
Here is a haiku
written under a minute
just because I can.

The Best Yet
Writing this shit now
in case work is too busy.
These are quality.

Bring It
I'm watching the sky
as it gets more and more grey,
just hoping for rain.

Losers
Yesterday at work
I saw a book of haiku.
It was weak-ass shit.

Haiku No More
When this book comes out
they'll retire the haiku
because I'm the best.

No Fucking Way
All those other dorks
trying to write haiku, like
they can do better.

Fucking Try Me, Bitches
It's not possible.
Just give up, haiku writers.
The Champ can't be beat.

HAIKU FUCK YOU

Food Haiku
Still pretty hungry.
Had a yogurt for breakfast.
My god, I'm the best.

Oh No, No Joe
Joe is at work now.
There's still time before I leave.
Fill it with haiku.

Ergh
Stomach is rumbling.
Should've had more than yogurt.
Oh well, no time now.

Possibilities is Endless
I could get pizza
or something else while at work,
besides the stuffing.

Crowds of Dipshits
Oh, but then again,
if town is really crowded
that's not the best plan.

Weird Slow Beasts
The people in town
don't know how to walk, I swear.
Not sure how they live.

Thank You, the Rain
Hey look, it's raining!
Keep up the good work, rain clouds!
Flush the scum away!

The Frankenstein Effect
The story's like this:
a joke that got out of hand,
but we ran with it.

Take It From Me
Haiku is easy.
Don't listen to naysayers,
listen to the Champ.

Make It Perfect
Beer, apple stuffing,
a rainy day in New Hope.
Don't fuck this up, life.

Sorry, Matt
I'm bad at email,
and worse at introductions,
but great at haiku!

Purple Shirt
Dig my purple shirt.
It's better than your dumb shirts.
Look at it. Fuck you.

Champ Shirt
Shirt fit for a Champ,
that's exactly what it is.
Duh, I'm wearing it.

Cloudy Day
It's kind of dark out.
Cloudy as all hell, really.
And me? I love it.

Opening
Closed at eleven.
Opening at ten today.
My brain is scrambled.

Late Night
Stayed up until one
watching *Hannibal* as well.
I'm running on fumes.

HAIKU FUCK YOU

So Many Books
Can't decide between
Joe Lansdale and Frank Turner.
I'm bad at reading.

Tattoo Madness
Got the itch again.
It's time for a new tattoo.
Maybe one for this.

More Cider, Please
Well, apple cider.
That'll start my day off right.
Joe is a dipshit.

Return of the Shirt
Purple shirt again.
You heard me, motherfucker.
Purple shirt for life.

FTHC
It's been a real joy
discovering Frank Turner.
Perfect tunes for now.

Ow, My Back
Propped up on pillows
attempting to write in bed
and losing to pain.

Hold Up
Sounds dramatic, huh?
Well, relax. I'm not injured.
Just uncomfortable.

Be Honest
I like honesty.
The best music is honest.
Even if it's shit.

HAIKU FUCK YOU

More On Honesty
Same goes for writing.
Be honest or be gone, yeah?
No time for bullshit.

Hint
Stacks of Lawrence Block
fell from shelves onto my bed.
Telling me something?

The Crime Novel Champ
I love Lawrence Block.
His writing is just flawless.
The man is a champ.

Tree Lighting
I left work early
to avoid the tree lighting.
They flip a switch, guys.

Chicken Scratch

My handwriting sucks,
but writing propped up like this
makes it total shit.

A Day's Work

Done writing for now.
I'll read for a little bit
and then go to bed.

Monday Morning

Woke up late again.
After a busy weekend,
I'd like a slow day.

They Can't All Be Gems

Looks like Christmastime.
Decorations everywhere.
This haiku is shit.

Paranoia
I hope Jen's not mad
that I left early last night.
I would have been stuck.

11:06
Some time before work.
Listening to some good tunes
and writing haiku.

Hi, Friend
Still a little shocked
that this project's a real thing,
and that it feels right.

Haiku Tattoo
Right around Christmas
I'll get my haiku tattoo.
That's decided, then.

Clarification Again
Now don't be confused,
I'm not getting a haiku,
but something for this.

That Dopey Little Smile
Ol' Angurgapi,
to stop barrels from leaking.
That's the fucking one.

Weird
Found I lost some weight.
I haven't been trying to.
Maybe I'm dying.

Still Weird
I'm not complaining,
I could stand to lose the weight.
It's just odd, is all

HAIKU FUCK YOU

Ever to Triumph
Late lunch at Triumph.
Fries and beer to save my soul
from Christmas music.

THEM FUCKIN' PRETZELS DUDE
Wait, slight change of plan.
Pretzels rather than French fries.
Everything is great.

YOU HAVE NO IDEA
Pretzels with cheese sauce?
You bet your fuckin' tits, mate.
Food fit for the Champ!

Chicken Tenders Are For Assholes
Fuck your tenders, Joe.
Pretzels are the best, you shit.
Fucking asshole twat.

How Bars Should Be
Bar's nearly empty.
Just me and employees here.
This is pretty nice.

Ginger Wildheart is a Fucking Hero
Shirt's too big today.
A Ginger shirt one size up,
worn for the great man.

WWMAD?
I often wonder,
"What would Michael Arnzen do?"
in terms of writing.

Monday Night
Another beer, please.
Oh wait, I'm the bartender!
More beer for the Champ!

HAIKU FUCK YOU

Brewsday Tuesday
It feels good knowing
I don't have work tomorrow.
I can drink lots now.

Plans!
Plans for my day off:
trip to Manoff's, write haiku,
read, read, read, read, read.

Josser Bank
Christ, *Market Harbour*
is great rainy day music.
I love that album.

DREEMZ
Fucked up dreams last night.
I'm not too fond of dreaming.
I much rather sleep.

Bestest Ever
Got nothing to prove.
No chip on the Champ's shoulder.
I'm the best there is.

Best Champ Best
I said I'm the best.
Did you miss that? Huh, punk ass?
Get outta my face.

Leave Me Alone, Please
Why, on my day off,
does everyone have to call
and keep me from it?

Right, Everybody Fuck Off
Just spent four long days
dealing with shitty tourists.
Give me one day, here.

Days Off Are For Suckers, I Guess
I just want to write,
go to the market, come home,
and read a damn book.

Overeasy
Nobody listens
when I tell them shit, you know?
The Champ has spoken!

Haiku Fuck You
Turn the music up,
write another dumb haiku,
and look at the rain.

Hat
I could wear a hat.
Yeah, maybe that would do it.
Let me get my hat.

Dog is Dog
Coop's jumping on me.
Maybe he has to go out.
But it's raining, dude.

Time Change
My sleep patterns have
changed significantly since
I started my job.

Patterns, Whatever
I stay up later
and wake up later and I'm
still not used to it.

It Isn't.
Joseph hurt his neck.
Maybe he'll die, ha ha ha!
Hey, that's not funny.

HAIKU FUCK YOU

Hat Update
So far the hat has
made my head go all itchy.
Um. Inconclusive.

CURDS
I just picked up some
roasted garlic cheese curds, yo.
That shit's delicious.

Sauce Life
Also bought more sauce.
Four fucking jars of the stuff.
Now THAT'S a haiku.

Grey Sky Smile
Rainy day today.
It's grey and dreary and great.
I really love this.

So Much Cider
More cider? You bet!
It's so good, I can't help it.
You fucking hippies.

Mimes
Haven't read today.
Too busy writing this shit.
But I'm almost done!

503
Just passed five hundred.
It feels weird to be this close.
Guess I'll keep going.

Chill
Wow, I just got cold.
Haiku Champ needs a sweater.
Oh my fucking god.

HAIKU FUCK YOU

Hip De Dip
First beer of the day,
a tasty winter lager
what I just done bought.

Atrocious
Joe is a disgrace.
Wore the same clothes for three days.
Unacceptable.

Fucking Swine
At the very least,
he could change his fucking shirt
so no one would know.

I'm So Angry
Do you hear me, Joe?
I'm writing about you and
your filthy clothing.

Lessons
It's not hard to change.
You just put on other clothes.
It's easy, you SHIT.

Disgusting, Hateful Child
I know that you own
more than one shirt, you fucker.
Go put one on. Now.

Disown
God, you disgust me.
Where did I go wrong with you?
You're no son of mine.

Change, Joe.
Change your fucking shirt.
Put on a new pair of pants.
For god's sake, shower.

HAIKU FUCK YOU

Fear and Also Fear
Knew this would happen.
Pen is almost out of ink.
Steady on, soldier.

A Birthday Haiku For J. David Osborne
J. David Osborne.
Your name has five syllables,
J. David Osborne.

Anyway
But back to Joseph
and his filthy fucking life.
Sort yourself out, Joe.

Threat?
Three days? You monster.
Change your fucking clothes
before I kill you.

No, a Promise
Overreacting?
I'm trying to help you, Joe.
Change or die. Simple.

I'm Mocking You, Dipshit
Blah blah duh blah fart,
I'm Joe, I wear the same shit
for three fucking days.

Near the End
Thirty-seven left
and my pen has given up.
Sleep now, my old friend.

Make Do
Can't find all the pens
I have in a box somewhere,
but this one will do.

Reflections
This close to the end,
let's see what we've learned, shall we?
Oh, that's right. Fuck all.

More Rain
Second rainy day,
but this time I have to work.
Today will be slow.

Wednesday, 12/02/15
Let's have a good day,
write some Champ-level haiku,
maybe grab a beer.

Oh, Shit No
Fucking customer
once referred to me as "kid."
I'm the fucking CHAMP.

A Friendly Reminder
Look at this shit, Joe.
You see how easy this is?
I'm not even done!

Goddamn, I'm Good
I wrote more haiku
in a couple weeks than you
will in your whole life.

Fuckin' Champ Can't Be Touched
That's why I'm the Champ.
I write haiku like the best
'cause that's what I am.

THE CHAMP STANDS DEFIANT
Half hour 'til work.
I could finish this right now.
I could. But I won't.

Best Food In Town
Tonight's dinner was
paneer makhni from Jaffron.
My soul is happy.

666
Marked my leftovers,
which I'll eat tomorrow night,
with a "Hail Satan."

Hail Hail
And a pentagram.
And two inverted crosses.
And blood from a goat.

Nah, Only Joking
That last part's made up.
I don't even have a goat!
And who gives a shit?

Charlie, Don't.
Charlie made a pun.
And it was about haiku.
It made me angry.

6:57
Rainy day at work.
Hardly any customers.
Just got déjà vu.

So Goddamn Close
Think I'll write the rest
when I'm relaxing at home,
unless I can't wait.

Mistakes Will Be Made
Leftovers might not
make it through to tomorrow.
Too damn delicious.

HAIKU FUCK YOU

Nothingface
Every other shop
is playing Christmas music.
We're bucking the trend.

An Hour Left
Beer when I get home.
Fuel for the final haiku.
Guess it has to end.

ESB
Just got home from work.
Got a beer, let Cooper out.
Now let's finish this.

Two Weeks
Joe said the deadline
was by the end of the year.
It just took two weeks.

Never Doubt the Champ!
Joe had no clue what
the Champ was capable of.
Behold the Champ's might!

Doubts Are For Suckers
If you doubted me,
don't you feel pretty dumb now?
This has been great, guys.

A Term For Being Too Contented
I've enjoyed myself.
It's been really fulfilling.
The Champ is content.

Old Friend
My foot is asleep.
It couldn't handle the Champ.
Rest now, foot. You're safe.

HAIKU FUCK YOU

Look At It
I'm not joking now,
this feels really fucking good.
I'm proud of this thing.

Success
It's pretty dumb, yeah,
but you know what else it is?
It's fucking honest.

Best of Three
Out of all my books,
admittedly not many,
this might be the best.

Effortless Majesty
Because, you know what?
This wasn't trying. This just
happened. I love that.

Bittersweet
And now it's near done.
I really think I'll miss it.
Not to get maudlin.

That Idiot
Hell, where else can I
talk this much shit about Joe?
That dumb fucking Joe.

Sort of Unbelievable
Wow. It's really here.
That number seemed far away
not that long ago.

Champ Forever, Champ For Life
But here it is, and
goddamn, it feels good to be
fucking Haiku Champ.

The Final Time?
I hope you like this.
I did. I fucking loved it.
Fuck off, Joe. I won.

Don't Be a Stranger
This was lots of fun.
Maybe one day there will be
Haiku Fuck You, Too.

555
So that's it. It's done.
Be decent to each other.
Champ, over and out.

The Haiku Champ would like to apologize to the following:

My family, Matthew Revert, William Pauley III, Stephanie Wytovich, Gabino Iglesias, Danny Evarts, Tommy Davis, Michael Nau, Casey Caracciolo, Gregory Bouthiette, Andersen Prunty, CV Hunt, Magen Cubed, Brent Carpentier, Scott Nicolay, Jonathan Moon, Michael Allen Rose, Jess Gulbranson, Grant Wamack, Kerry Cullen, Shane Cartledge, Sam McCanna, John Edward Lawson, Jennifer Barnes, everyone at DogCon2015, the Fat Friar, the Farley's Bookshop Crew: Charlie, Buffy, Caitlyn, Julian, Michael, Jen, and Rebekah, Team 555, Tim Smith, Ginger Wildheart, and all other bastions of weirdness and sanity in a strip-malled world.

From the Haiku Champ: Music He Writes Haiku To And Now You Can, Too

Sing to God — Cardiacs
Virion — The Sequence of Prime
England Keep My Bones — Frank Turner
No Help For the Mighty Ones — SubRosa
Christ Send Light — Nadja & Black Boned Angel

ABOUT THE HAIKU CHAMP

Josh Myers is the author of *Feast of Oblivion* and *GUNS*. He lives in Lambertville, NJ, with his dog, FBI Special Agent Dale Cooper. He works at Farley's Bookshop in New Hope, PA, and operates Carrion Blue 555 with Joseph Bouthiette Jr., which is the only reason this book exists.

CATALOGUE BLUE 555

CPSIA information can be obtained
at www.ICGtesting.com
Printed in the USA
BVHW07s0724161018
530284BV00003B/41/P

9 780996 276801